To:_____

From:_____

Date:_____

The Jesus With Us Series is dedicated to showing children how much He loves them and that He is always with them. This awareness will develop faith and confidence, paving the way for a brighter future.
— S&L

Copyright © 2022 by Sybrand & Lucia. All rights reserved.
Published by Ciana Publishers.

This Book is Copyright Protected:

This is only for personal use. You cannot amend, distribute, sell, use, quote, or paraphrase any part of the content within this book without the consent of the authors. The Authors guarantee all contents are original and do not infringe upon the legal rights of any other person or work.

No part of this book may be reproduced, duplicated, or transmitted in any form by means such as printing, scanning, photocopying, or otherwise, without direct written permission from the authors or publisher, except for the use of quotations in a book review and as permitted by the U.S. copyright law. For permission, contact info@cianapublishers.com.

Disclaimer and Terms of Use:
This book is provided solely for spiritual upliftment, entertainment, motivational and informational purposes.

All Scripture quotations, unless otherwise indicated, are taken from the Holy Bible, New International Version®, NIV®. Copyright ©1973, 1978, 1984, 2011 by Biblica, Inc.™ Used by permission of Zondervan. All rights reserved worldwide. www.zondervan.com The "NIV" and "New International Version" are trademarks registered in the United States Patent and Trademark Office by Biblica, Inc.™

Authors - Sybrand JvR & Lucia S

cianapublishers.com

THE RHYME OF THE UNFORGIVING SERVANT IS BASED ON MATTHEW 18:21-35

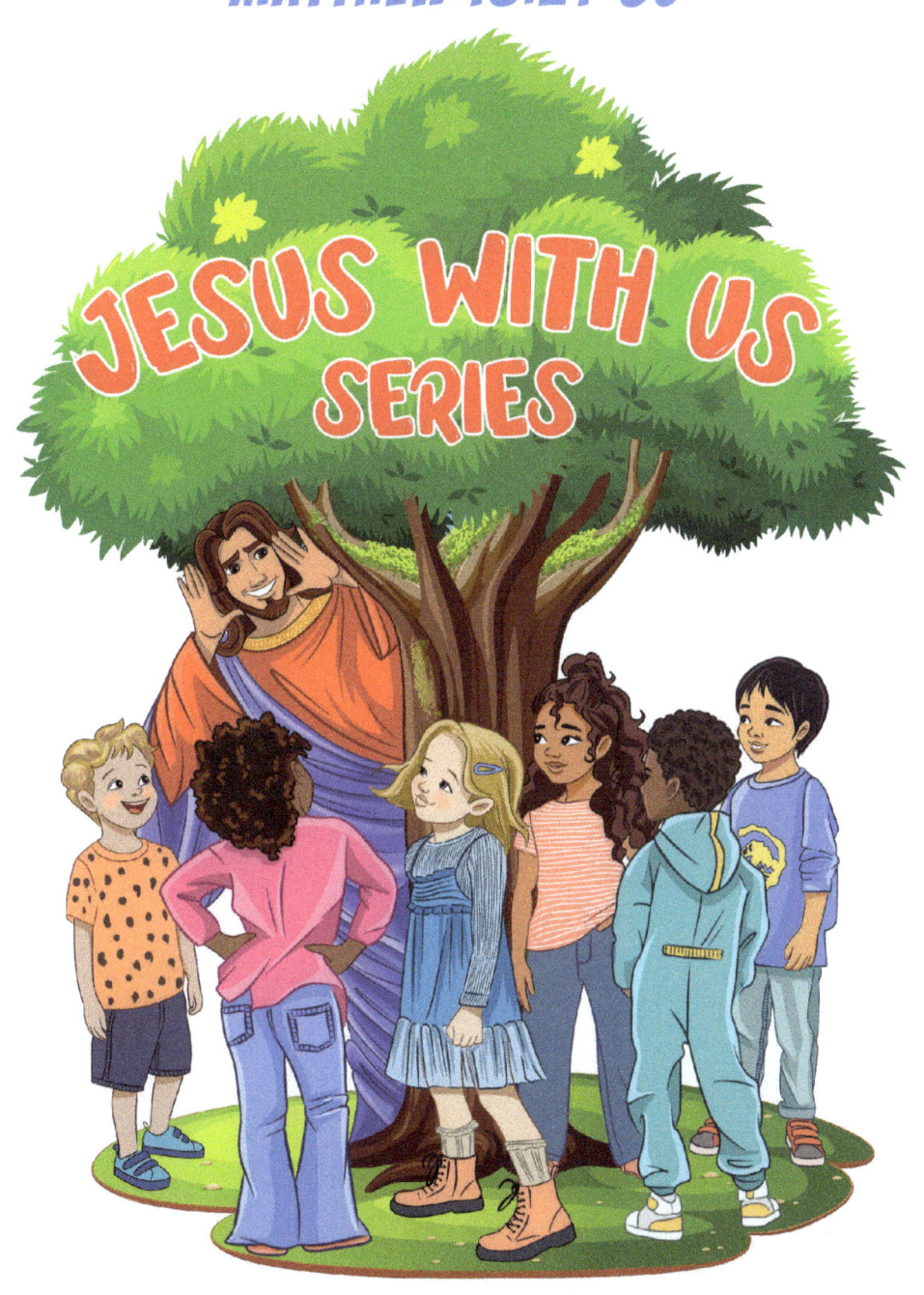

There was a king who wanted back his gold.
He told his servants, "Pay up or be sold!"
They brought a man who owed ten-fold.

On his knees, the servant begged and cried.
"Forgive me, my king; I've really tried."
"Have mercy; your servant hasn't lied."

The servant's pleading touched the king's heart.
"I forgive your debt, go and make a new start."
"Get up, live your life, and in peace depart."

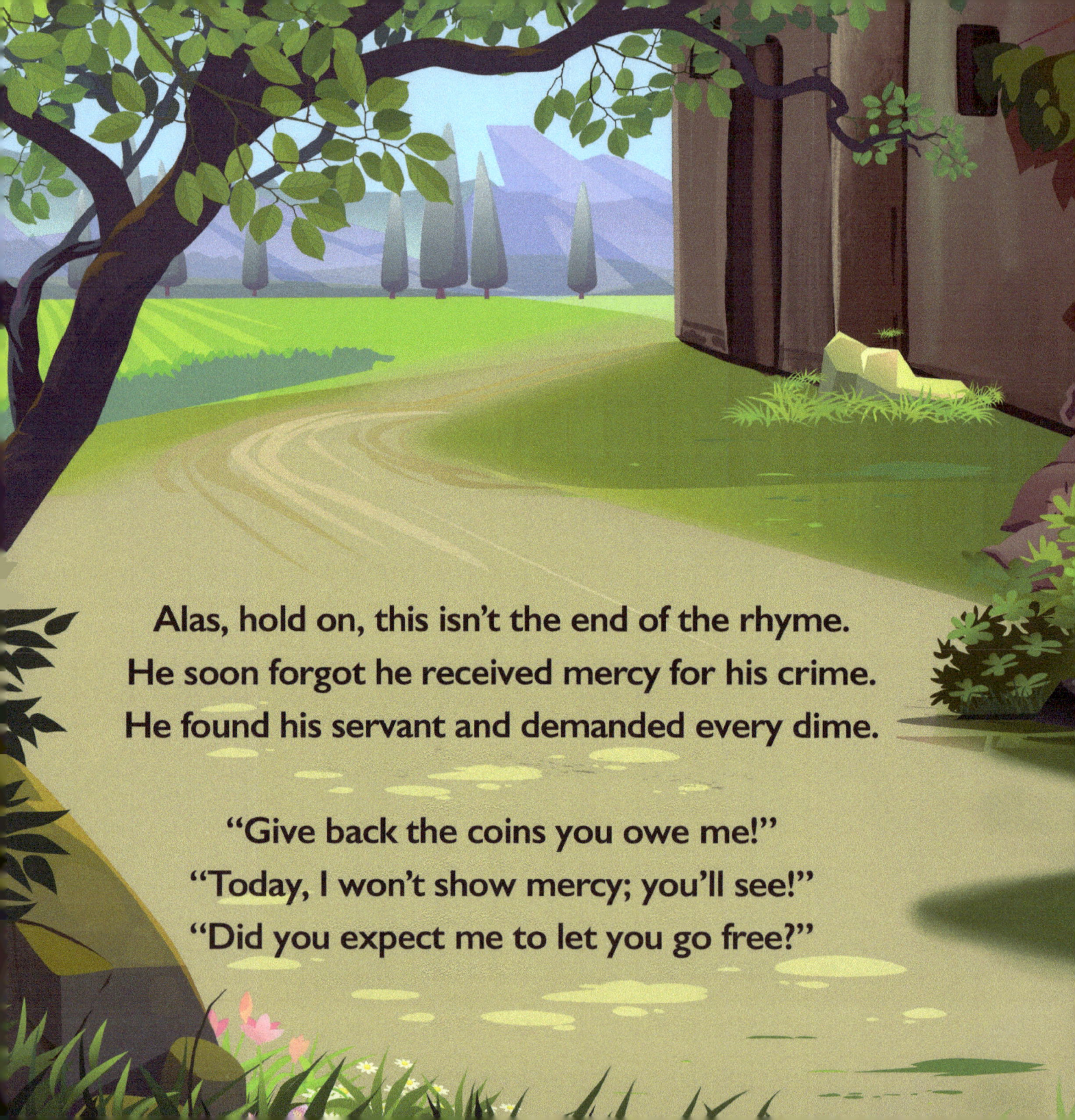

Alas, hold on, this isn't the end of the rhyme.
He soon forgot he received mercy for his crime.
He found his servant and demanded every dime.

"Give back the coins you owe me!"
"Today, I won't show mercy; you'll see!"
"Did you expect me to let you go free?"

With teary eyes, the servant fell to his knees.
"Sir, right now, I can't pay back your fees."
"I'll return it. I need more time, please."

The Unforgiving Servant's anger had risen.
He shut his ears and refused to listen.
"Call the guards; throw him in prison!"

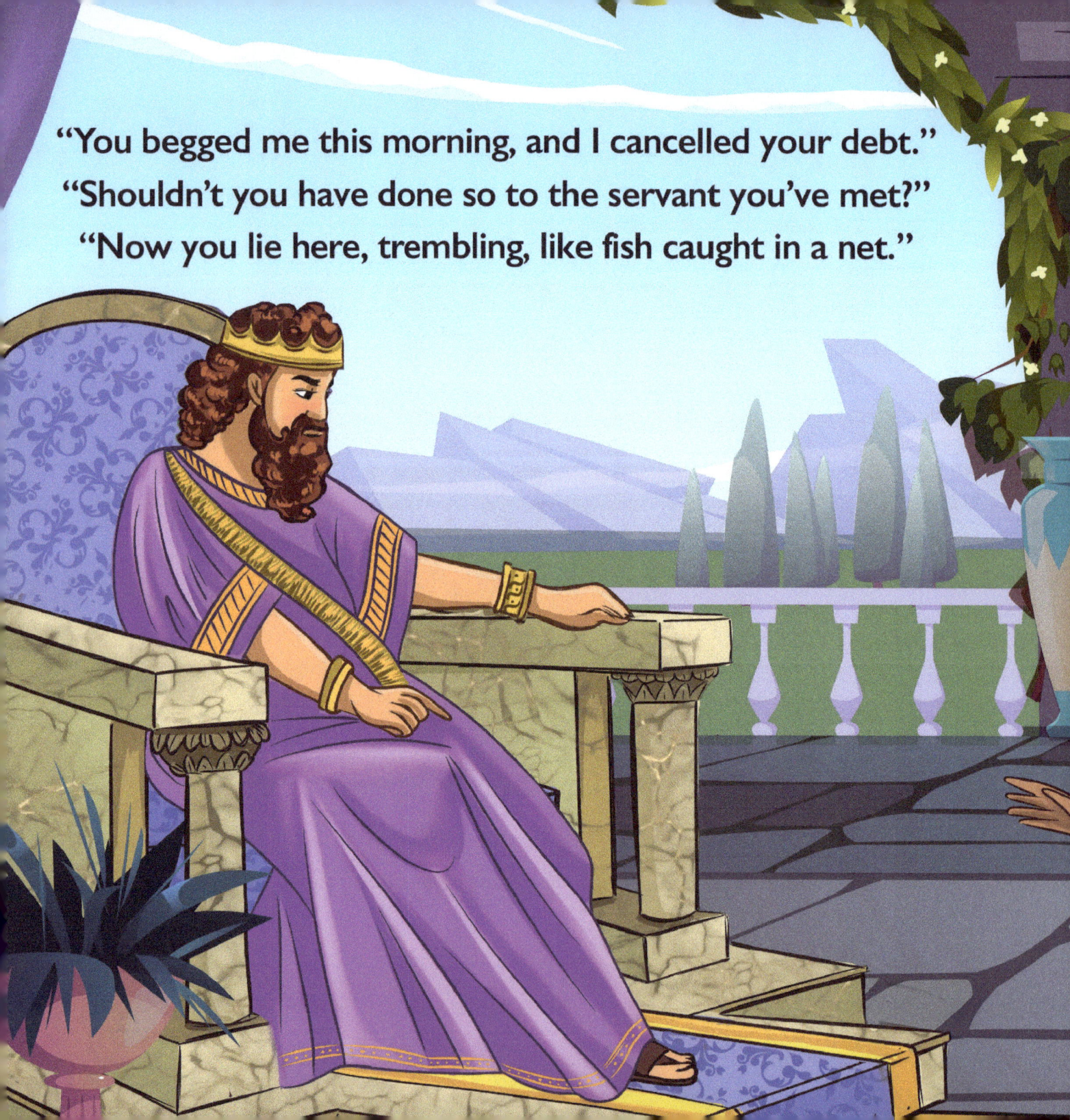

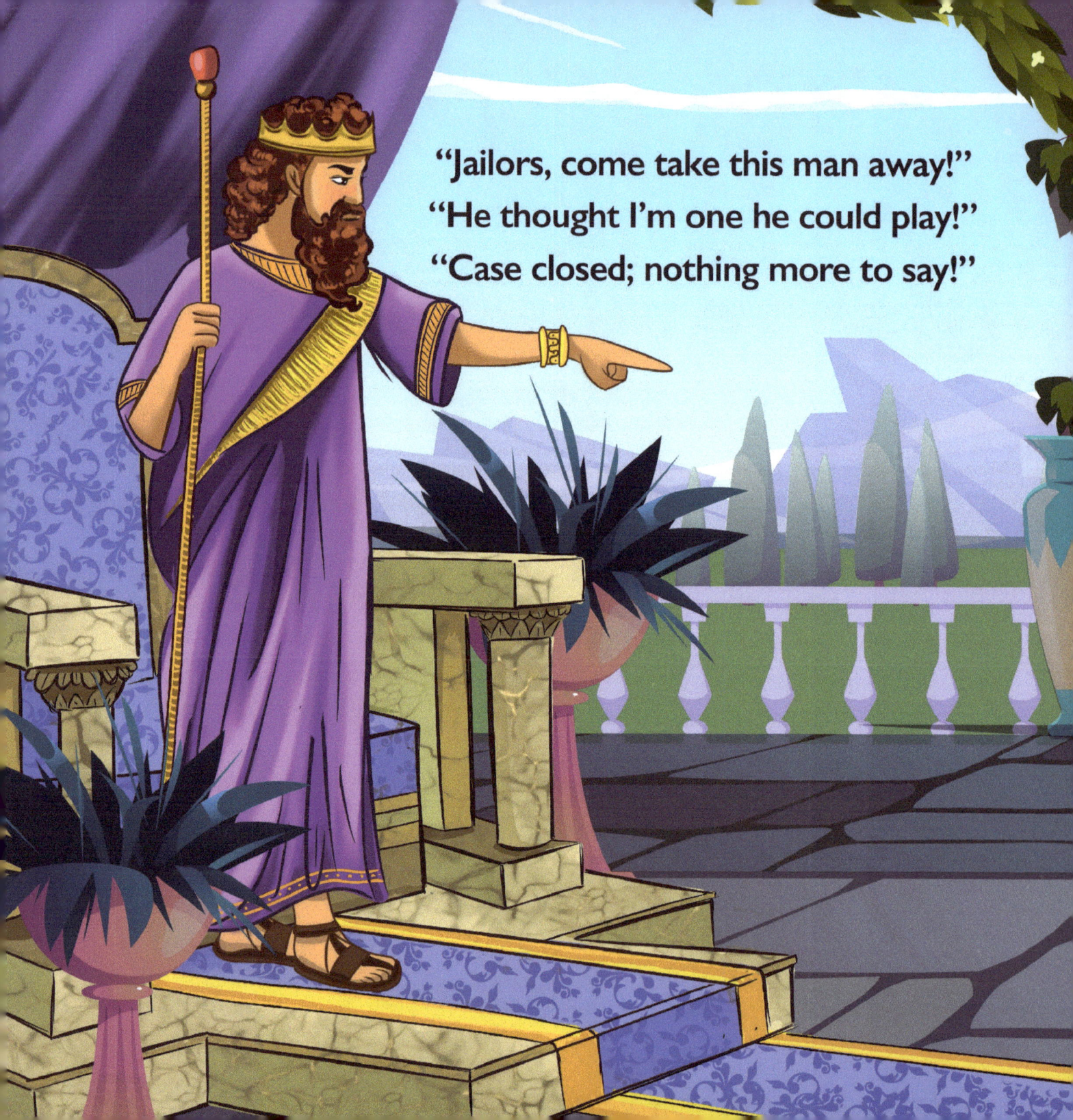

"Forgiveness or unforgiveness; by which are you driven?"
"The Unforgiving Servant was set free and forgiven."
"Not forgiving, he lost the freedom he was given."

Praise the Lord!
Do you forgive those who wrong you?
Others will wrong you, and you will wrong others.
The Lord's Prayer in Luke 11:4 NIV says,
"Forgive us our sins, for we also forgive everyone who sins against us."
We need to be forgiven, and we need to forgive.

The king forgave The Unforgiving Servant.
In return, The Unforgiving Servant didn't forgive his servant.
As a result, The Unforgiving Servant was put in jail.

If you know that stealing will put you in jail, you will not steal. In the same way, you will be quick to forgive if you know that not forgiving someone puts you in jail. I mean, not forgiving others locks us in a prison of anger and hatred. Forgiving others sets our hearts free from anger and hatred.

Jesus lives in your heart, and when you don't forgive others, unforgiveness, too, lives in your heart. Jesus wants to be the only One who lives in your heart. Through this parable, Jesus emphasises that as He forgives us, we need to forgive others so our hearts can be free for Him alone.

Tell somebody: "Forgive and be Forgiven."

Lord Jesus Christ.

Make Your home in my heart.
And help me to play my own part.

Help me to forgive as You are forgiving me.
Remove anger and hatred, so my heart can be free.

In Jesus' name.

Amen! Amen! Amen!

MATTHEW 18:25-27, 32-34 NIV

25 Since he was not able to pay,
the master ordered that he and his wife and his
children and all that he had be sold to repay the debt.

26 "At this the servant fell on his knees before him.
'Be patient with me,' he begged,
'and I will pay back everything.'

27 The servant's master took pity on him, canceled
the debt and let him go.

32 "Then the master called the servant in.
'You wicked servant,' he said, 'I canceled
all that debt of yours because you begged me to.

33 Shouldn't you have had mercy
on your fellow servant just as I had on you?'

34 In anger his master handed him over to the jailers
to be tortured, until he should pay back all he owed.

FOR FURTHER READING: MATTHEW 18:21-35

LET'S CHAT

What can you say about how The Unforgiving Servant treated his servant? _____
_____
_____

How could The Unforgiving Servant have shown appreciation after the king forgave his debt?
_____
_____

Do you remember a time when you were forgiven? How did it make you feel? _____
_____
_____

Why is it important to forgive others? _____
_____
_____

Why do you think the king threw The Unforgiving Servant in jail? _____
_____
_____

Is there anyone you need to forgive? _____
_____
_____

When you forgive, you are set free from anger and hatred. Do you agree? _____
_____
_____

WORDS IN THE RHYME MADE EASY TO UNDERSTAND

Parables:
Stories told by Jesus to teach us how to be good and to tell us more about His Kingdom, His Father, and Heaven.

Ten-fold:
In the rhyme, 'ten-fold' means, 'They brought a servant who owed the king ten times more money than the other servants.'

Grace:
In the rhyme, 'grace' means, 'Although The Unforgiving Servant didn't deserve it, the king has given him enough time to pay back the money he owed.'

Bestowed:
In the rhyme, 'bestowed' means, 'Giving someone a gift. The gift the king gave The Unforgiving Servant was grace.'

Bellowed:
In the rhyme, 'bellowed' means, 'The king shouted with a loud voice.'

Mercy:
Mercy is when you receive forgiveness. In the rhyme, 'mercy' means, 'The Unforgiving Servant begged the king to forgive him.'

Touched the king's heart:
In the rhyme, 'touched the king's heart' means, 'The king felt sorry for The Unforgiving Servant and cancelled his debt.'

Debt:
Something, typically money, that is owed.

Alas
In the rhyme, 'alas' means, 'Something bad is going to happen. There is more to the story.'

WORDS IN THE RHYME MADE EASY TO UNDERSTAND

Dime:

In the rhyme, 'dime' means 'Money or gold.'

Anger had risen:

In the rhyme, 'anger had risen' means, 'The Unforgiving Servant became very angry.'

Boss:

In the rhyme, 'boss' means, 'The king.'

Offspring:

In the rhyme, 'offspring' means, 'I have treated you like my own son.'

Trembling, like fish caught in a net:

In the rhyme, 'trembling, like fish caught in a net' means, 'As fish are stressed and fighting to get out of a net, in the same way, The Unforgiving Servant was scared and shaking.'

One he could play:

In the rhyme, 'one he could play' means, 'The Unforgiving Servant thought that he could treat the king like a fool, because he begged and received forgiveness, but thereafter he didn't forgive his own servant.'

Forgiveness or unforgiveness; by which are you driven:

In the rhyme, 'forgiveness or unforgiveness; by which are you driven' means, 'Are you quick to forgive or are you slow to forgive and rather stay angry?'

Lock you in a prison:

In the message, 'lock you in a prison' means, 'When your heart is filled with anger and hatred, it is like being in prison because your heart is not totally free for Jesus as He wants to be the only One who lives in your heart.'

OTHER BOOKS IN THE JESUS WITH US SERIES

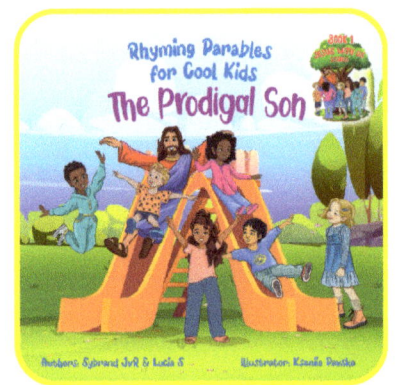

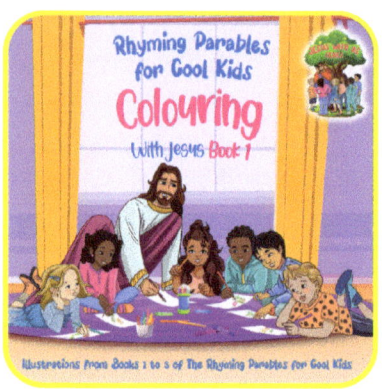

OTHER BOOKS BY THE AUTHORS

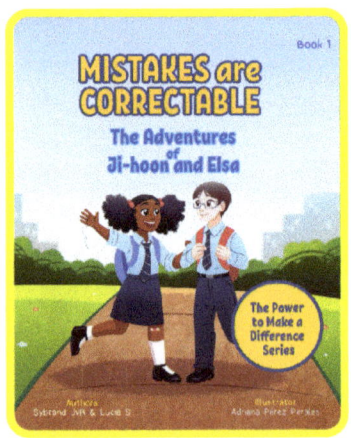
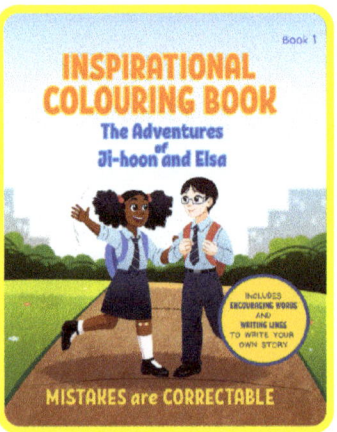

www.ingramcontent.com/pod-product-compliance
Lightning Source LLC
Chambersburg PA
CBHW042030100526
44587CB00029B/4361